Read-About® Health

Food Safety

By Sharon Gordon

Consultants
Nanci R. Vargus, Ed.D.
Primary Multiage Teacher
Decatur Township Schools, Indianapolis, Indiana

Jan Jenner, Ph.D.

Children's Press®
A Division of Scholastic Inc.
New York   Toronto   London   Auckland   Sydney
Mexico City   New Delhi   Hong Kong
Danbury, Connecticut

Designer: Herman Adler Design
Photo Researcher: Caroline Anderson
The photo on the cover shows a child checking a milk carton to see if the milk is safe to drink.

Library of Congress Cataloging-in-Publication Data

Gordon, Sharon.
    Food safety / by Sharon Gordon.
        p. cm. — (Rookie read-about health)
    Includes index.
    Summary: Discusses the importance of safely preparing and storing the foods we eat to maintain good health.
        ISBN 0-516-22294-5 (lib. bdg.)   0-516-25988-1 (pbk.)
    1. Food adulteration and inspection—Juvenile literature. [1. Food handling—Safety measures. 2. Safety.] I. Title. II. Series.
TX531 .G67 2001
363.19'26—dc21

                                                    00-047367

©2001 Children's Press®
A Division of Scholastic Inc.
Printed in the United States of America.
1 2 3 4 5 6 7 8 9 10 R 10 09 08 07 06 05 04 03 02 01

Look at all the food!

4

Eating good food helps you grow strong and healthy. But eating bad food can make you sick!

How can you tell if something is safe to eat? Use your senses.

Look at food carefully.

If it looks rotten, it probably
is rotten. Throw it away!

Sometimes you can smell if food is bad. Sour milk smells terrible!

Pour it out!

Never taste food that
you think might be bad.
Show it to an adult.

Do not ask someone
else to try it—not even
your pet!

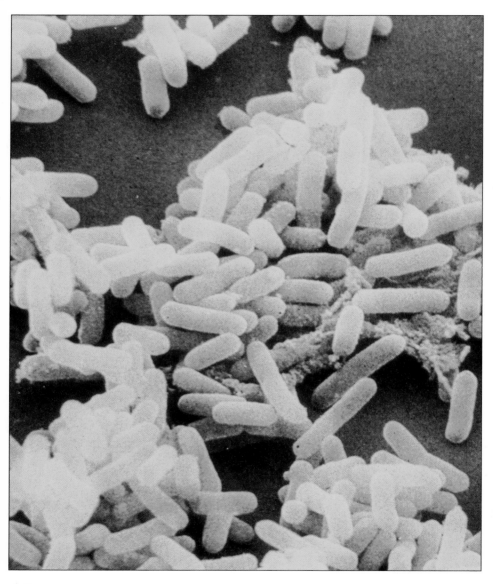

12

Good food goes bad
because of bacteria
(bak-TEER-ee-uh),
or germs.

Germs are tiny living
things. They are in your
food and on your hands.

Some germs can make
you sick.

Always wash your hands with soap and water before you eat. Washing gets rid of the germs.

There are germs on fruits
and vegetables. You need
to wash these foods before
eating them.

There are many germs
in uncooked meat.

Do not touch it. If you
do, wash your hands
right away!

When you eat meat, make
sure it has been cooked
long enough.

Do not eat hamburger or chicken that is still pink. Well-done is the safest!

Always keep hot food hot.
Keep cold food cold. Keep
frozen food frozen.

21

Make sure your dishes are clean. Wash them in hot, soapy water. Then rinse them well.

When you go shopping
with your parents, read the
label on the food you pick.
It tells you if the food is
still fresh.

Do not pick cans with dents.

Do not pick packages that are open. Do not pick eggs that are cracked.

When it comes to your food, just remember— it is better to be safe than sorry!

Words You Know

cold food

frozen food

hot food

rotten food

30

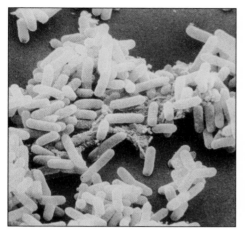

bacteria

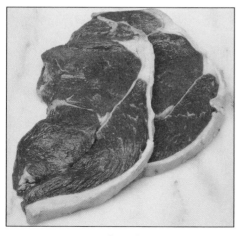

label

uncooked meat

soap and water

Index

About the Author

Sharon Gordon is a writer living in Midland Park, New Jersey. She and her husband have three school-aged children and a spoiled pooch. Together they enjoy visiting the Outer Banks of North Carolina as often as possible.

Photo Credits

Photographs ©: Mandy Rosenfeld: 8, 9, 11; Photo Researchers, NY: 29 (David M. Grossman); PhotoEdit: 3, 6 (Bill Aron), 19, 22 (Tony Freeman), 18 (Michael Newman), 14, 15, 20, 30 bottom left, bottom right (David Young-Wolff); Rigoberto Quinteros: cover, 27; Stone: 17, 31 bottom left (Tom Main); Visuals Unlimited: 4 (Bill Beatty), 7, 30 bottom right (Jack M. Bostrack), 25, 31 top right (Jeff Greenberg), 21 bottom, 26, 30 top right (Gregg Ozzo), 12, 31 top left (D.M. Phillips), 21 top, 30 top left (D. Yeske).